Copyright © 2018 Doug Stanfield
Gatekeeper Press

gatekeeper press
Where Authors are Family

All rights reserved.
ISBN: 9781642371949
eISBN: 978164237195

Table of Contents

Dedicated… 5

Acknowledgments........................6

Trouble Comes..............................7

Folding Power 8

Not Jesus in A Popup Camper ...10

Pause...15

Umwelt..16

Summer Sounds 18

The Waters 19

Innocence 20

Vows...21

The Cork's Dilemma 23

The Water: A Ghazal 25

At the Dig......................................26

Time and Memories....................27

Pipe Organ Mud Dauber 29

Hometown Heroes......................32

Tick, Tick..33

Upstream is a Dream..................34

Song of the Hidden Moon 36

On the Verge 38

Vacation..39

Time Traveler................................41

Nothing to See Here 43

The Work 44

Six Dogs..47

Finding Bottom 48

Bringing In The Tide....................49

Waiting in the Dark......................50

The Ticking of the Clock 51

Time and Mountains 52

I Was A Horse 55

Einstein Lit A Cigarette 56

Pin Me Slowly...............................57

Deadline..58

Seven Six-Word Stories 60

Solid Things..................................61

Hitting the High Notes 62

Ghostling In Training 63

The Water Cycle 67

Breadcrumbs in Rapids 68

Ordinary Things...........................70

Illusions 73

Invisible Travelers........................74

Alley Time.....................................76

A Prickle of Hedgehogs 79

Sanctuary.......................................80

Expensive Mistakes 81

In The Beginning.........................83

Thunder Comes............................85

Hunger...86

Hope 87

We've Done What Was Asked....88

Yes 89

The Gods Must Change 90

Grace is a Verb.............................91

Woman...92

Sacrifice 93

Ride the Cresting Salt 94

Wonder 95

Dance the Dawn...........................96

The Hanging Road.......................97

The Future is Pregnant..............102

Celebrate the Temporary 103

Effort and Simplicity 104

And So It Begins Again.............109

Ordinary Days 111

Lazarus, After 112

Epiphany 115

Mileposts 118

Endings..119

Dedicated…

…

To this brief journey of life,

to this bittersweet, time-traveling adventure;

to the utter absurdity of our

helpless, daily leap into the future;

to all the surprises and pain;

To all ironies, all injustice, all waste;

all discoveries, all mysteries, all loves,

all heartbreak, all joys.

Come, then. Sit with me a while.

Let's drink some wine and

share our joys and sorrows.

Let us celebrate the temporary and

Let go of what will not last …

For even the perfect snowflake melts,

and every precious thing turns

to ashes under the sun.

Acknowledgments

<u>Influences</u>

    Jim Harrison

    Carl Sandburg

    Jim Gardner

    John Lennon

    Joni Mitchell

    William S.

    Charles Bukowski

    Paul

    Billy Collins

    Marcus Aurelius

    Princess the Wonder dog

    and above all,

    Wilda Farrell Stanfield (1947-2018)

<u>Poems from "Snowflakes and Ashes" also appeared in</u>:

    Spillwords Press (various)

    Austin Poetry Festival Anthology

    hemmingplay.com

    Poets Corner

    Poetry Breakfast

    The Tele-poem Project

> *My special thanks to Sally Heffentreyer and Jeff Hermann for help with editing and design. But despite their best efforts to protect me from myself, errors remain. These are all mine.*

Trouble Comes

Tinged like mercury,

Like the edges of old coins...

Trouble comes.

Folding Power

I asked for the superpower of "Folding" for my birthday.
It cuts out the middle man:
Gimme a calendar with tricky bits, I said.
I'd fold weeks, months, years, centuries together,
jump to any time, past or future.
The first would be hanging with
the first human band to walk out of Africa .
I'd wait in the shade of a date palm, by the Nile,
bounce rocks off crocodiles, watch the south trail.
I'd cook hot dogs and hamburgers,
have beer chilling on ice.
History's first tailgate.

I would show them an iPhone, photos, movies.
Order something from Amazon
Wouldn't that be a trick!...
Maybe a slinky, some bows and arrows and knives.
A chemistry set. Aspirin. Cargo pants,
broad-brimmed hats and sunglasses.
Trail mix. Snickers. Matches.
A stainless mug. A mirror.
Triple antibiotic cream.
It's in our interest that they survive the trip.
I'd tell them to be kind to one another,
Let them think I was the Great Spirit, then disappear.

I would fold a map of earth upon itself

again and again, touch this place

with Nebraska,

with California, or Istanbul,

Melbourne, Bali, Borneo—wherever you are.

Just touch two dots together

and be there, no jet-lag.

Or I would take my

super-power-star-chart and touch

this place to one halfway across the

galaxy, or another galaxy, or Jupiter

or a planet with an atmosphere of pure joy.

I'd pause to take in the light show

of the Pillars of Creation,

birthplace of stars,

then fold again,

take a left at the second star and go on

'til morning to

Never-Never Land,

find the Lost Boys,

buzz Captain Hook,

share a joint with

Tinker Bell and

pray I

find my way back.

Not Jesus in A Popup Camper

I am astonished.

Home after 50 years on the road,

I've had mainly ordinary disappointments.

It wasn't all Jesus in a popup camper,

riding along the Hanging Road....

but it was all right.

If I had a fireplace,

I'd build a fire and sit

With a big-eyed Labrador I don't have,

and an imaginary cat or two—

one on the mantle, one in my lap—

And flip through the memories,

Sipping brandy and smoking

a pipe I also don't have—

Since I quit smoking.

I have wiped the spider webs from the door

Cleaned the musty rooms

Thrown out that rotten food left in the 'fridge.

Cleaned the basement and attic of

Things that don't matter.

(And maybe never did.)

There's still more to do,
But the old place waited patiently,
and now is livable.

I was away longer than planned,
Living under the perverse and immutable rule of
The Universal Law of Unintended Consequences,
The intent statement says:

> *"It shall be impossible to control everything.*
> *Even if you somehow are delusional enough*
> *to believe, against all evidence, that*
> *you control <u>almost</u> everything, or*
> *Nearly everything —*
> *more than anyone ever has,*
> *more than anyone ever will — "*
> *There will always be something you miss.*
> *Always.*
> *Take that to the bank.*
> *And just because the Universe is*
> *bored and thinks it's*
> *fun to mess with you,*
> *This one thing will be the thing*
> *that screws you over.*
> *Every time, boy-o.*
> *It's the law. Deal with it."*

The trip? Ahhh, yes. That.

A long, loopy, spastic waking fever-dream,

Out around the sun, a slingshot back, coasting through

The cold void and the silence, alone,

To Mars and her moons, and back again,

To the past, to the future, and landing in the present,

Only to cross wilderness and water,

Barren desert and lush mountains.

Guess how much of that was on purpose?

The whole thing was shot through with wanting and

Emptiness and hidden vibrations and distant lights,

Filled with many corners, inevitable surprises around each,

And over and over, I met myself, wanting.

There was no end of wanting.

Understanding little but driven by wanting.

The sea moves always, the wind moves always,

I want and I want and there was no end to it.

Now? I just want time to sort things.

The forms are completed, the reports filed.

I am free. One manacle after another has been cut away.

I have nothing useful to do,

and no one to tell me to do it anyway.

I walk the buckled sidewalks of the old neighborhood,

The children and I listen to the birds

In the trees sing like crystal then soar free.

We imagine we fly with them,

High above the Earth.

This new home life will take some adjustment.

I don't know the lingo any more,

The streets have changed,

The unhappy couple next door got old, died,

And the kids living in their house

Give me wide berth,

Laugh and run away,

Shouting in an alien,

yet faintly familiar language.

Inhabiting the skin of my

most advanced age yet is

The strangest feeling, sometimes.

Inside I'm still young, curious, horny and wistful.

Still wanting, but not sure

What would satisfy the need.

Then I look in the mirror and see

A stranger — with mileage,

a certain baffled weariness...

but me .

I wish I could grow one magic eye,

Able to see the truth of things,

And not despair.

But maybe I found a seed of it on the trip,

And while it needs a little tending,

There is occasionally some magic in it.

Everything I've done, everything and everyone

I've known; the friends, the enemies;

The broken bodies I left in my wake;

All the times I failed to just be kind,

Or to learn from my mistakes,

If any of it had been different,

Even something small I didn't notice at the time,

The story would have been entirely different.

Somewhere in South America,

A butterfly flaps his wings

The Universe laughs with me.

Pause

I have left my old house,

In a manner of leaving…

So to speak

You might say….

But have forgotten where the new one is.

This would be inconvenient

Any other time.

But not now. I'm used to the feeling.

Now I know to pause.

Stand here for a moment,

Have a drink. Pet the dog.

Listen to the sound of the big creek

Scraping patiently along the banks

In November when the land is bare.

Not caring where it goes, or why,

Just behaving according to it's nature

Carrying the secrets and

Dreams we toss in upstream,

Whispering its own back to us

Washing fish and mud and secrets

From here to somewhere else.

Maybe it will tell me

How it is I might be more fully myself.

Umwelt

Some days it's all about limitations,

And while it's no use complaining,

That's never stopped me before.

I feel like a blind man living inside a kaleidoscope;

A glutton with but one taste bud left;

A monk who's forgotten what he knew of God;

A tin-eared drunk waking up just as angels

burst across the heavens in song.

I'm a coma patient wrapped in wet wool,

strapped in a closet in an unlit room

in the back of the basement.

The blind tick only cares for

butyric acid's smell,

and the exact temperature of blood.

When it senses these things

it lets go of the twig and

falls into blackness. Sometimes

it will land on the fur,

feed on the blood

of a passing deer.

The small part of the world it senses

is its *umwelt*. Nothing else is real to it.

Nothing else needs to be.

For the black ghost knife-fish, it's electrical fields.

For the echolocating bat, it's air-compression waves.

For us, it's a narrow band of the electromagnetic spectrum
our eyes are adapted to see, the wavelengths
that have the highest energy in sunlight.
The colors of ripening fruit and food, as it happens.

Our other senses are just good enough to get by.
We can't compete with a bloodhound's
olfactory genius; we're pitiful in that department.
Such is our *umwelt*.
We sense a tiny sliver of the world.
We don't know anything more,
Our *umwelt*, out of which
we construct everything
like a sacred myth…
what we think we know,
what we sense,
what we fall toward,
hopeful,
in the dark.

Summer Sounds

Cicadas, and the birds that hunt them.

A neighbor's lawnmower.

The whisper of the maple leaves in a cool morning breeze.

A dog, barking for show somewhere over there.

A catch in the air, ever so faint, a momentary pause.

News of the first real cold front coming down out of Canada.

The fat rump of late summer has settled in, humid and hot.

But if you listen--and if you tend to see the

rain cloud in every silver lining, like me,

You sip your morning coffee and listen harder,

feel the breezes more,

Because we know in our bones that everything moves on,

That only a fool would have lived his life in hard pursuits

Without realizing that all these moments

Come once and are gone,

as surely as it is that

heavy ol' Summer

Will struggle one day soon and

move on south, making room

For other precious and holy moments

that need attention,

as this one does.

The Waters

The water rubs the stone

Soft and cool, or fast and hot.

Day upon day.

The stone's contours shift and soften

Day upon day.

Stone surrenders stone in cautious ways,

To become a mountain in the ocean deep someday.

10 million years is as nothing to the stone,

Or the water, rubbing each other

day by day by day.

There is no place on Earth water cannot go

And where water goes, it changes things.

There is no place you cannot go.

The sharp edges always dissolve,

Reappearing in new arrangements, new places

Conjured by the patient, soft rubbing of water.

Rubbing the contours smooth,

Dissolving one thing to patiently build another.

Day upon day upon day.

Innocence

Everyone but God, if you believe, is

Innocent of tomorrow.

Caesar, full of swagger,

innocent of the daggers of friends,

Mary, innocent a son would be murdered,

slowly,

while she watched.

Me, innocent about everything, including

whether a satellite will fall on me, or if

I'll get a certified letter that

immortality, six virgins and a chocolate cake

will be delivered on Saturday by 10 a.m..

I struggle to reconcile ignorance and innocence.

Do I care about what I can't or don't know?

Do I need more than this one, infinite moment?

Meanwhile, they say the snow will stop soon.

In a world of white, quiet and cold,

finches empty the bird feeder

and wait for more.

I am still innocent of Spring.

Vows

I was 21 when I took the official vows,
but had really taken the important ones
some months earlier. When I proposed
on April Fools Day and she said 'yes.'

But vows are merciless things, and they don't
tell you the whole story. You can't listen, anyway,
with your eyes full of hunger for each other
and your ears full of music and laughter and stories.

It's easy to make grand promises when you
don't know all that will be asked of you,
the blood and the bone and the grief.
You find out the truth bit by bit,
day by day. You find out
where you're weak and where strong,
and whether you're someone people
can count on.

But you never learn these things unless
you have solemnly vowed,
and then **kept** the promises
made in hope and ignorance.
You learn the lessons that come
only with walking a long road,

until your feet are worn as thin as paper

and the dust of the road is your new skin.

And, if you're lucky, keeping promises

has, with much practice, become second nature.

I found all this out the hard way.

I slept for 50 years, more or less,

but when I awoke, it was

to shorter days and cool nights.

And with promises to keep.

The Cork's Dilemma

Spring is so fast, so eager.

Changes come before I've absorbed yesterday's.

A minute ago, the maple was nearly bare,

thousands of tiny spinners fallen on my windshield

like sawdust under a table saw.

This morning, new leaves dance in the breeze,

awkward teenagers already,

swaying to their own music,

turning the bright sunshine green.

Have I missed something important?

I wish the world had a rewind button,

or at least a pause option.

But sadly, we drift along like a cork in a stream,

never knowing what's down below,

never staying anywhere.

Only able to see a blurred impression of the scene whizzing by.

So, yes, I'm torn between the ineffable beauty of now

and the endless wonders

around each bend of the stream.

I cannot slow the stream, but have learned a trick:

I pause on my own, breathe deeply, still my mind.

When I eat, I will really taste the food; savor the wine.

Miss no opportunity to be kind.

See the joy in another's eyes.

I'll watch the young leaves dance and try to
imagine the smiling lips of the wind.
And when I laugh, it will be from the soles of my feet,
and when I'm sad, I'll not be afraid to plumb the depths.
And when I love, I will hold nothing back, even
When, as is inevitable, there is pain.
I'll observe more and better.
That's all I can do.
That's all any of us can do.
After all, we'll be dead soon enough.

The Water: A Ghazal

I was a relentless swimmer as a child, more at home
under water, popping up only for air, wishing for gills.

*In the pond a few feet down, the big bass, motionless,
eyes swiveling, waited for someone's last mistake.*

In the muddy shallows, the sun warmed the water most,
small things hatched, safe from mouths in the deep water.

*Forests of fronds and grasses stretched toward the light,
and died, becoming the black ooze where biting things lived.*

I lost that simple way a child observes in wonder,
accepting in wisdom, the heavenly song of the world.

*My job these days is to be the archeologist of my life, diving
over and over and staying down, wishing for gills.*

On soft summers nights, lovesick bullfrogs boom at the edges.
A muskrat's wake in the moonlight; stones and fields, asleep.

At the Dig

I see a soft brush
in my mind's hand,
clearing the dust.
I was six or seven,

and we were at recess at
the old school building.

The day glowed under a high blue sky
in the last warmth of late October.
The girls squealed and ran
—*just fast enough* to get
caught while the boys were interested—
Learning the rules of the mating game.

The yellow maple and bright-red oak
leaves grounded in wind-shaped drifts.
Farm kids, we asked a teacher for the rake
we made piles, big soft piles
and jumped in them while Mrs. Fish looked on,
her arms crossed, sharing the moment,
stretching recess a few minutes because she knew
moments like this would end soon enough
and we would be gone...

Time and Memories

Time and memories intertwine

like a ball of earthworms.

Who knows where one starts

and the other ends?

They say we cannot remember things

before a certain age.

We may see pictures and know

we were alive earlier, but that's just

the picture album version of life;

the real switch in us is still not on.

Mine came on when I was two-something years old.

My parents tore down the old chicken house.

It was in the afternoon of a slightly cloudy day.

I had a coat on, so it must have been

still early in the year. Late March, maybe.

The grass was the vivid green of brand-new.

Old boards, stained with decades of chicken lives,

ended in a pile that would be burned.

Dust and old feathers floated free

from hiding places.

A fixture in my world changed.

This is my first memory.

My dog guarded me, stayed by my side until
the demolition exposed a rat's nest.
She smelled them, knew the danger.
She attacked with a speed and ferocity
that was both thrilling and scary.
There was a brief, violent battle
with inhuman screams, then silence.

She came and sat beside me again.
She knew her job.
Kept me safe with no doubts.
And I learned the difference
between life and death.
The switch was on.
And I knew at once
why the grass was so green.

Pipe Organ Mud Dauber

Shimmering metalicelectricbrightblue armorskin,

Wire-waisted,

Twitchy, angry wings

Searing sting, like hot death.

Oh, yes. I learned.

Mud dauber wasps drop

Out of the sun like Messerschmitts,

All angles and crackling danger.

They landed at the muddy edge of the pond

Like a strike of cobalt lightning

A stance that said "this beach is mine!"

Like aliens from Saturday morning TV,

Flung angry from the heart of some magenta sun.

They scan for danger and get to work.

I watch from a safe distance,

Study how they stalk over the

Narrow band of workable mud at pond's edge,

Wings and antennae twitching,

Cocky, threatening, angular, busy.

They *were* picky.

Not just *any* mud would do, apparently.

But prime mud, from the waspish Goldilocks distance from the water

—"Not too wet, not too dry, just right"

Rolled into little balls and

Flown to a hand-hewn beam
in the ancient barn
with the bark still on one side.
.

Again and again and again and again.
Until the nest, like a pipe organ,
Grew on wood cut when U.S. Grant was
writing his memoirs
at the Jersey Shore.

Once the pipes were built,
The wasps hunted spiders,
Paralyzed them with a sting and
Stuffed them in the tubes
to feed their babies.

The mysterious waters
fed my soul, gave me the world of
mud, in the grasses and weeds,
Where nature breathed, bred and
died in all her bloody glory.
Life everywhere, raw and clear.
Even in a drop of water,
magnified in a microscope
given to me, life struggled.
In the mud, disturbed, tiny monsters squirmed.

I swam out to deeper water,

Observed, mesmerized,
Where the big bass and turtles hid,
Algae and long, languid grasses grew.
Dragonflies, snakes, water birds,
Frogs and salamanders tried to hide.
I learned about survival and habitat,
How different places shelter larvae, tadpoles, minnows,
Or snakes or three kinds of turtles
Leopard or bull frogs or toads,
Egg clusters of frogs; dragonflies, and their
Murderous underwater larval form, the nymphs;
Dead things, decaying, consumed, reused.
It was a wondrous panorama.

What strange beauty it was to see
muskrats swim, silently,
Making a v-shaped wake on the surface
On a summer's night under a full moon.

But it was always the blue mud daubers building
Their silent grey pipe organs
I watched most.
Like virtuoso soloists flown in from Budapest
While the house orchestra played on behind.
Part of the elegant and vast symphony revealed
On the muddy banks of childhood.

Hometown Heroes

All around town hang
lamppost banners in memory
of hometown heroes.
Boys in uniforms who went to war
in 1941, or '42 or '43 or later,
who never came back from that
sunken transport ship, or that
awful night on Iwo,
or who stepped in front of a truck
outside a bar at 1 a.m. in liberated
France, having dodged all the bullets
but not a truck full of supplies.

Maybe people who live in
mountain towns like this
Just have longer memories than most,
surrounded by the rounded remnants
of a once-great mountain range.
Rocks have long memories.
Or maybe we have a need to hang
onto deep things longer than is fashionable
in these fast, temporary times.

Tick, Tick

The ticking of a clock is the

sound our blood makes

as it ducks out the back door of today

and takes the bus

to yesterday.

A clock creates

the illusion that everything

is controlled by

even, orderly forces.

But there is always the

last 'tick'.

Then what?

I counted to ten, and

with each count I dropped a

stone in the stream.

The stones all sank

but the circular memory of each moved on,

evenly spaced,

stone became water,

cause and effect,

separated by time.

Upstream is a Dream

Time is a deep river with a fast current,
the past somewhere upstream.

You can try to swim against the flow,
but it's no use. It's exhausting, and pointless.

You can't go there any more.
You might taste a memory,

But are soon worn out and
forced to tend to more immediate problems.

Just let the water
carry you along. It's much easier.

You hear the shouts and cries of others.
The banks are near and sharp.

The past is out of sight and
mist hides everything downstream.

The water is white and turbulent.
You can't see the rocks and drowned snags until you're
right on them. Then it's up to luck and leg strength.

Sometimes you miss them, sometimes they get you.
Sometimes the screams you hear are your own.

But always the flow is strong, and pushes down,
through unseen things into the future.

Song of the Hidden Moon

Without fail, monthly, the full moon sheds
her inky cloak of night and stars
and slips a leg and then the rest into the lake,
her cool fire subtracted from the sky.
She leaves the nights more lonely, barren.
But her life is not extinguished,
merely hidden, recovering, re-energizing.

She must withdraw from sight,
make herself desirable, let her belly be lush and fertile again
so she may breathe passions onto the world, be
drunk with the reckless, raucous, ribald dance of life.

She rolls overhead, silver ship of the night sky,
goddess of the oestrus cycle,
of "οἶστρος", *sexual desire.*
We await her return with blood singing,
Lashed by desires we do not comprehend.

She reappears, rising from the ocean's depths,
playing her cool blue light on
the backs of cavorting whales,
pulling ten million squid to the surface,
sending flying fish soaring across the waves,
driving life into a frenzy of mating and
feasting and dying around the world.

Then she sways seductively up rivers,

up small streams and higher on rocky slopes until,

reflected, refracted into trillions of tiny droplets

on every living thing,

she leaps back into the sky, resplendent,

and spreads her seductive waves of

gravity across the face of the world.

Women sigh in their sleep and stir,

their skin flushed from the friction of moonlight,

in sleep, they squeeze hands slowly between thighs,

their water nature filling the night air,

sending out a call of longing and promises.

Men grow restless, querulous with each other,

hungers grow, urgency grabs hearts

stirred by the slender fingers of cold blue gravity.

We are pulled out into the night,

into the dark where truth and secrets can be shared,

and the urge to feel the

welcoming touch of another,

the healing intimacy of "I see you,"

becomes overwhelming, a need

unspoken, demanding completion,

reflecting in a happy joining,

the hidden language of the moon.

On the Verge

I'm on the verge.

You just wait and see.

I was young, once.

Didn't know what I didn't know,

Below average in basketball, baseball,

sat on the bench;

And full of endless, vast, gaping,

gnawing caverns of ignorance.

But I also harbored a dumb stubbornness,

And that made the difference.

So now I'm a burden on everyone,

cashing that Social Security check, living the dream.

I might use all this free time to

write the untold history of the doorknob, or

invent the inexpensive, irreplaceable

solution to all your problems.

Oh, yes. That.

I'd make millions, billions, and buy a Greek island

Full of sun, ruins, waterfalls and nubile goddesses,

and do something really great, then.

So great.

You just watch and see if I don't.

Vacation

After 60 years of work, more or less,

I've decided to take a working vacation.

I'm booking a cruise and extended

train travels for the next 60 years

To go exploring along the coast,

Poking my canoe up the inlets and rivers,

Probing the veins and wires and memories of

Unfamiliar parts of me, to

See whether there's anything

Worth saving.

I hope to sit down at a cafe, occasionally,

Order hot, strong coffee and a bag of beignets,

Look sufficiently safe and vulnerable and mysterious,

Have a young Cajun girl with dark eyes come over,

Take a chair and steal one of my pastries,

Smile and flirt and tease with her youth and beauty,

Kiss me like she means to make a habit of it and

Say she finds me interesting enough for that, and not creepy.

(Old men's dreams never tire of that one.)

The old chess pieces are all there, still covered in blood.

Time eats us alive and today I am one day older

Yet still younger than tomorrow.

I'll get back to you about next month.

I am set out on an uncertain enterprise,

With uncertain plans and unknown consequences.

Save me from myself, Oh Lord,

The cry in every throat.

Usually ignored by God

After so many sincere failures.

Time Traveler

You know the bit about the butterfly:

It flaps its wings on a Wednesday afternoon and

the dinosaurs all die?

And the other bit, where you go back in time

and accidentally bump off great-grandpa

and POOF! You never existed.

Or just like yesterday, and you woke up,

decided on grapefruit instead of your usual egg,

and you felt good enough to go out instead,

and managed to find and kill Hitler.

You time traveler, you. You did it again.

What might have happened, didn't.

Something else did.

We play a game with babies

Put a cloth over her eyes,

"Where's daddy?" Then whip

away the cloth and he's back.

Things exist that we cannot see.

We imagine we move through time because

Our brains record memories

And recall them "later".

But that's because we're used to seeing

from inside the action,

where things don't happen all at once.

In the mind of God, outside of all of this,

In the realm of pure thought,

Everything has already happened.

Past, future, now have no meaning,

nothing changes because

everything, *all-when*, already is.

Change is mere illusion depending

on where you stand and watch.

Weird, isn't it?

A world where

butterflies can kill dinosaurs,

where what you see

depends on where you stand,

where traveling through time

is what we all do, every day,

and we don't even know it.

Nothing to See Here

There's really no point in another poem about Spring.

What can be said that's new?

Well, nothing

Just that this year it seems the lilacs

fill late April's dusks with

their perfume in intoxicating ways...

and the idea, however brief,

that this year, this year... will be remarkable,

remembered in our old age

as the one,

the one the lilacs predicted.

The Work

The old one-eyed poet said it is harder to
dismantle your life than to build it, but
I think it is just as difficult both ways.

I'm putting the finishing touches on the house of me.
Bolting the copper wind vane
shaped like a leaping trout on the chimney,
mounting the mailbox by the road,
putting in the shrubbery and sod, laying out the welcome mat.

And doing it all never knowing if today
might be the last, or whether I have
6,200 more sunrises to enjoy, as I saw once in a dream.

It's all just vanity, after all. I'll pile my collection of rocks
beside the trail and someone will come along and
knock them over, not realizing what they are,
then steal a few to build their own pile.
These are not unusual worries and really
only concern me and a distressingly small circle of people.

The Nile River doesn't care either way, Miami and
San Francisco and Shanghai are still going to flood,
people will always believe flim-flam artists,
the dinosaurs are still dead.

This life-sorting–patching-filtering
feels like falling asleep on a muggy
afternoon and waking up sweaty,
disoriented, not sure where – or who — you are.

The Work, though, goes on.
It means to remember things, to patch torn screens,
To oil squeaky hinges of faintly remembered doors,
To somehow put a name to things and to see
What actually matters and which bits were bullshit.
(There has been a *lot* of the latter.)

The woman behind me on the train is coughing,
reminding me I read once
that most of us die of suffocation,
Choking on our own accumulated miseries.
I can think of better ways to go.
She makes me start coughing, too.
And so I write it down.

I'm putting the finishing touches on my life,
Essentially sewing my shroud. I'm not unhappy about this,
Mind you. I'm luckier than most, and get to do the
Necessary sifting and sorting. I have time for the Great Work.
Then it will be time to dismantle it all, brick by brick,
Board by board, while I have the strength.
I'm not panicking or being morbid, either. Just realistic.

I have the luxury to know what it is I need to do.
I'll pack it in neatly labeled boxes and files. I'm lucky.

I get to tell my story, leave these words behind as an affidavit
And testimony in my own very ordinary voice—which will last
About as long as a certain pile of stones, I suppose. But
It's the effort that counts. The making use of a life
To learn what one can. To leave a small mark behind.
And then to let go, and see where the current goes from here.

BITS AND PIECES
Six Dogs

He often thinks of the

six dogs who ran alongside

for a time and then were gone.

All those afternoons of

poking noses together into

interesting places, and

not having to explain why.

These honored companions

deserve to be cast in bronze and

mounted facing the wind on

granite pedestals, on a river bank

beneath old trees,

Nodding, 'ah, yes, these were noble friends.'

Let's honor them like Civil War heroes

on the field at Gettysburg.

Each cemented tight to the heart of things that were important,

Things that only dogs and children understand.

BITS AND PIECES
Finding Bottom

Old pilots say:

"There are more airplanes in the ocean

than submarines in the sky."

The sea hides everything forever,

The wind strokes her face.

Everything finds the bottom in time.

Every other expectation is

Self deception,

Pleasant, perhaps, but

still a lie.

BITS AND PIECES
Bringing In The Tide

Peaceful inside this train, quiet, rolling through South Carolina at midnight, gently rocking side to side, as smooth as the hips of a woman strolling to dinner on the boardwalk on a hot July evening,
Thin fabric stretched just right
over just-so-right curves.
Making him wait,

Liking the feeling she gets from the way she walks, knowing she just made a guy crash into a rack of postcards.

Her rhythms are as old as the ocean, in time with the waves out in the musky duskiness of another hot day, Both bringing more good things to shore.

The seagulls cry overhead. The crowds of tourists part as she passes.

Bits and Pieces
Waiting in the Dark

Just after sundown,

past the North Carolina border,

our passenger train stops to let

a freight whiz by in the dark.

We're not as profitable per pound,

and complain when the ride's too rough.

And, really, just look at us; so flabby and soft.

So we must wait.

It's good to know your value in

this big, wide world can be

calculated in weight, wholesale price, and volume.

But the delay has already been factored in.

It's just how this is done.

For the first time in my life I'm

comfortable waiting, in the dark,

a mere human, one of billions.

The Ticking of the Clock

We sat by the fire and you put your bare foot in my lap.
I was looking out the window, lost somewhen,
then whisked back to the now by the
insistence of the slenderest of ankles.

I came later to find you asleep, naked, on your stomach,
Hair spread across the pillow. I
uttered a silent, joyful primal prayer.
Then, as things are in dreams,
 we were moving, connected, content.
But the moment was ripped away.
You faded quickly and in a moment gone,
all but an impression of the slenderest of ankles,
hair on a pillow, and the ticking of a clock.

Time and Mountains

The time was, we thought we had a handle on time,
but our time here is so short that there's no
time to really understand what time is--
or even if we ever will.
There just isn't enough of it for anything.
The pharaohs sat their fat asses
firmly on a people who could not
remember a time before this curious arrangement...
before those arrogant bastards arose
who thought they knew best,
who were so clever with grain storage
and gods and stone,
who thought the world worked best
as a pyramid with them at the top.

In the times of the pharaohs,
time had a different meaning...there
in the dull, slow heat of the desert
in between floods and plagues and
the brief, beautiful springtime.

The parasites tricked the people—
who were bored and out of work
and likely to cause trouble—
into stacking millions of

blocks of rocks in magnificent piles as if

to say to the gods,

"See, we can build mountains, too!"

It also proved the Pharaoh

had the right to be in charge

since no one wanted to go to the trouble

of tearing all those rocks down.

But where are the pharaohs now?

Like real mountains, their piles of rocks will

end up as grains of sand,

blowing across the expanse of eternity

until they drift against the

base of some other fool's temporary monument.

I once had an uneasy relationship

with time, in the personae of clocks.

I couldn't wake with the sun, or sleep when

it got dark, and my soul was always

out of sorts, and anxious.

But at least everything didn't happen

all at the same time...

They say time-keeping changed when

railroad people needed to make things work

across vast distances. For commerce.

Speed made organization and precision necessary.

Then factories needed everyone to begin

making things all at the same.... time.

There's that word again.

I don't worry as much about clocks any more.

I let the computers keep track for me

and watch time rush past as if

in a hurry to join its siblings in the distant past

where it can get away from clocks.

There it can sink back into the black

cloud of being, where everything has already happened.

I Was A Horse

I woke up this morning from a dreamy grey half-sleep

with the February rain dripping off the eaves.

A memory floated by that in a previous life

I was a horse. No question.

A big, brown horse with

big, knowing eyes.

I had been abandoned

out in the high desert by someone,

but didn't care about them at all.

I knew once how to be free,

and would just do that again. I wondered

about finding water and something to eat,

but horses don't waste a lot of time worrying.

We're afraid of things that move,

and afraid of things that don't.

But we're smart enough to pick a

direction where it smells more like

water than not, and begin again.

Einstein Lit A Cigarette

Einstein lit a cigarette

and watched the violent violet

and lethal pastel afterglow

of the first atomic bomb

fade over the desert.

He inhaled,

a psychedelic and

highly addictive smoke—

and including

a bit of radioactive dust—

and wondered,

frowning, if God

ever had second thoughts.

Pin Me Slowly

Pin me, slowly,

With your softness,

your curves and deep desire.

Share with me

your liquid fire.

Then I will

coax from your throat

sighs, and grateful prayers to

the wisdom of a loving god.

Deadline

I dreamt of a place, not long ago, and the dream, unusual for me, showed even the most mundane things in vivid detail. Clothing, clouds, leaves on the ground, birds against the sky, dust motes floating by in super high definition.

But not at first. At first I was in the dark, walking blindly on a long journey through a wood. I only knew that something big was ahead. I was expected. It was my show.

I'm a modern plebe, raised on science and skepticism and American mythologies. But the longer I've lived, something far older has pushed me against things I cannot understand.

All through the night unlit by moon or stars, I sensed movement all around, a rustling of hurrying things. As though the trees of the forest were on the move, striding and jostling without words, just the sounds... the creak and flex of branches, and the whisper of air through leaves.

When I arrived at the designated place, they were already silently in place, and the air was hot and moist with expectation.

I was eager to find out what all the excitement was about.

What would make the forest wake and walk?

In the way of dreams, I just knew…this was some years from now. I was at a certain age. The gathering was of people in my childhood home town, most long gone, but now just as I remembered them.

They expected me, and gave a warm welcome.

You may wish to make something psychological of the imagery. Be my guest. I would be tempted, too. I don't mind.

But in this case, something is different.

I choose to believe that this was simply a moment of grace. I was given a glimpse into the future, given to know in advance how long I have. And it seemed quite a generous figure.

The joke could be on me, of course, and Jung and Freud could have a field day with the plentiful neuroses they could find in the symbols. Perhaps. Perhaps not.

However, I've always worked better under deadline. No truer term could there be, but it is soothing, somehow. That's part of who I am. It may just be as simple as that.

Now, if you'll excuse me... I must get back to the work.

Seven Six-Word Stories

"Get lawyer. Cops found the bodies."

"One bullet. One head. Two dead."

"House for sale: Divorced, discouraged, deactivated."

"Damn! Why are the walls moving?"

Captain: "Y'all ever flown upside down?"

"One sunrise left."

"Looks like rain."

"No trespassing here. No warning shots."

Solid Things

I need to find the grace of solid things,

wood, glass, stone;

to go below the surface,

hunt unique songs

locked away long ago by

water, earth or fire.

What the mind conjures,

free-floating and insubstantial,

needs to be balanced by solid things

that reveal

their compositions

when seduced by humility.

Hitting the High Notes

I write a bit younger than I am,

but my voice

cracks on the high notes now.

I don't know how much longer I can fake it.

I wish I had a daughter, who would sit and

listen and forgive me in the

way only daughters can.

Instead, I sit with my laptop

facing a bank of windows with a

view of a mountain,

snow flurries in the sun.

I'm encountering many me's, from many times,

in various stages of becoming.

It's as though I walk into a Greek amphitheater

in Corinth, and my many selves are sitting on the old blocks

of stone, twitching, and I point to one and say.

"OK, come on down. Today's your turn to whine about your life."

And we all lean in, ready to pounce,

evaluating the honesty, the growth,

knowing that one of us

will be judged next

and found wanting.

Ghostling In Training

There are more things in heaven and earth, Horatio,
Than are dreamt of in your philosophy....

I didn't think it would be like this.
I could have been convinced, mind you, But I was skeptical, in a benign
way. Unmoved except by facts, I said.

"Show me a ghost; I can't take your word for it. Let me talk to just *one*,"
I'd say to earnest believers, knowing they could not.
Show me. Prove it.
I even went looking on my own.
We once camped at Gettysburg when my sons were 8 and 10
I wanted them to visit such a place, to get a tiny taste of
The grand sweep of events, even though they were too young
To grasp much, and were more interested in lightning bugs
And climbing on a cannon or two.
As I recall, it was a humid, sticky summer night.
That typical time in July when the night stays hot
Well past midnight, the air coming up straight out of the Gulf
With humidity so high it's like breathing
Through wet gauze, or the exhaust of a clothes dryer,
The air full of bugs, bats and the mating calls of frogs in a boggy spot ...
And the occasional owl's hoot-whooo through the mist.
It was the kind of night you can feel the Earth
Pulsing, moving, breathing, desperately fertile; you can feel the
Sudden small deaths in the grasses, feeding more life.

I imagined as the night before the battle decades before,
A spooky night, pregnant with meaning, deadly and glorious,
Full of shadows and fears, of the clank of muskets and of men crying.
I couldn't sleep... too hot, too curious,
So once the others were asleep, I walked.
The crunch of gravel underfoot gave rhythm to the cicadas' song,
All along a blueish-silver path, with pockets of mist rising
I passed many monuments, frozen glories, massive in the gloom.
Down a grassy slope to a ridge, then beyond, to a low stone wall,
I looked out over rolling fields glowing in the moonlight.
Pickett's thousands had died out there, and more, all around.
I stood by the low stone wall, a place of horrible, desperate endings,
Once littered with bodies and gore and wreckage and screams, but
Resting quietly in the humidity of a July night.
But I neither saw nor felt any unhappy spirits.
Of all places, you'd think there would be at least one.
I listened for them, with my ears, with my doubting self.

A coyote trotted across the far edge of the field,
A single cloud skittered across the moon, casting deeper gloom.
All I got that night were a few mosquito bites.
It went on like this for years. Me, skeptical, waiting,
expecting nothing, getting nothing.
Until my body died (under circumstances I'd rather not go into). Let's
just say that it was 'messy.' And, much to my surprise, I'm still here.
Sort of. Enough of 'me' to dictate these words into

another's dream, at least.

For how long?

Until I can figure it out.

So I try to keep as busy as one can when you can't touch the world and

can only observe the world through a thin, scratchy barrier that makes

everything look like an old newsreel.

But things are different in many ways.

I listen in on people's conversations,

And drop in wherever and whenever I want.

Time and space are no longer limited as they were,

I visited my own past, and while I found some answers,

I came away from that feeling that my own existence

Was only ordinary. Was I a treasured child of God as I'd been taught?

I still don't know. God hasn't told me.

Maybe, though.

I have so much to learn.

Having nothing better to do, I spy on people:

Satisfy my curiosity about certain people, and strangers,

Listen to their conversations, and,

If the cosmic wind is right,

To their thoughts. It is all open to me now.

And yes, of course! I watch them flirting, lying,

flattering, cheating, having sex,

It was one of the first things I did in the early days.

(And if people aren't actually doing it,

They're mostly thinking, scheming about it.

We humans are a horny bunch, that's for sure.)

It was just...not as interesting to me in my new condition.

So I drifted off, disconcerted, a little disappointed,

but relieved, somehow.

I started listening more deeply to the ebb and flow

Of life beginning and life ending;

Of an ocean's-worth of desire and striving and defeat;

Of confusion and loss and sadnesses;

Of happiness in small things, and contentment.

It is no blessing to see things as they really are

But to no longer have any part to play.

And yet.... through it all, I learned....

What I used to call time passes. I feel some of it still

I am finally becoming a part of all I see.

Step into the undiscovered country.

Everything that was, is and shall be,

All that I see, all the others, present past and future,

are really parts of me.

And with that, I am a ghost no more.

The Water Cycle

The soul

Of the Water Cycle

Is in the eternal leveling of

Everything.

Operating in deep time,

Beyond the span of human empires,

A single drop of water spends

3,230 years in the ocean,

Then rises on the winds, floating free

For months, years, until it runs

Into the rain catcher claws of the mountain.

And inch by inch, mile by mile,

Hour by month by years by centuries….

It falls, always seeking

The ocean again,

Pulling the mountain down

With it.

Breadcrumbs in Rapids

The sound of a train's horn somewhere in the valley at night

Creamy thighs flashing

under a summer dress,

cool and molten at the same time

The smell of coffee when the sun's

just over the mountain.

A robin hatched by the kitchen door,

back in the yard,

hunting, says 'hello'

The look of an old door, the view out a window,

an old house that shelters me

Fireflies in June that send me

to a more innocent time

Old places, ancient sorrows,

hot winds across a desert far away

The way a tree moves under the

hand of an invisible thing

The way the sun sometimes comes up like thunder,

The cacophony of voices-- lonely, lusting, lost--

thinking they're the only ones

A dream, impossible, conjures up a past life, of running in the jungle,

finding a monk

Good times, lifelong loves, the joy of hearts connecting,

Seeing the ordinary and, for the first time,

opening to the extraordinary…..

All....

Breadcrumbs cast on a moving stream, floating on...

Ordinary Things

Ordinary things be time machines,

Containing important futures.

Surprising links to before-times.

A cardboard box that held a cheap microwave,

This morning.

Taking scissors to slice along the seam of the bottom,

Pulling to break the hold the staples had,

Breaking it down.

I was 16 again, back in the storeroom

Of the S&H Green Stamps store in my hometown,

My first real job.

I unloaded semi-trailer loads of stuff,

Stuff frugal people would order from catalogues,

Or walk into the store to buy with their

Carefully saved booklets of stamps.

So, I unloaded trucks, unpacked these things and

Put them on warehouse shelves

On the days when the trucks made deliveries

In the alley behind the store.

I learned what the backsides of ordinary things looked like.

My boss taught me how the world worked.

She told me what it meant to work, be there on time,

Tolerated my teenage awkwardness, trained me bit by bit,

Was firm when I failed, gentle when I tried, smiled when I needed encouragement,

Showed me how a business ran.

Talked to me when things were slow,

Let me know that adults had problems, too,

Told me stories about lessons she'd learned about

Marriage, about living. I still remember one thing,

That helped me later on. I knew it was important then, and

Held onto it somehow.

"No matter who you marry, and how much in love you are,

There will be days when you look at that person and wonder

'what in the world did I see in them?'

The important thing is what you do next," she said.

And chuckled with a hint of sadness.

She did that from time to time, and laughed at herself, at life.

Shaking her head, and getting back to work.

That's where I learned life was in the living, moving through it.

In cardboard boxes and shelving and in the company

Of older, kinder, competent people.

I wish I could remember her name.,

But I can see her face like I was 16 again.

She taught me how to do a job, made me better, scoffed at my bullshit,

Was real and practical and beautiful.

So when the trucks came on Wednesdays,

I unloaded them, trucked boxes inside,

Unpacked and stocked the shelves,

But the last thing on those hard days was to take a knife,

Slice piles of boxes apart and change them into flat things,

Ready to be removed, their function served.

No longer holding someone's precious

New microwave, or tool kit or sheets made of Egyptian cotton,

Ordinary again. But so much more.

Illusions

Chase we, all,

Things that glitter and shimmer,

Things that slither up against us,

Like a lovely someone in a short skirt on a street corner,

Smelling of perfume and friendly virtue.

Yet even when our desires are met

We are unfulfilled, more hollow than before.

Who knew we could sink even more?

Phantoms dissolve, mocking

Such foolish mortals as we.

Such an old, old story.

Two roads diverge in a yellow wood,

And by taking the one most traveled by,

Can we ever

Retrace our steps, and take that other path.

The truer one,

The one that could make all the difference?

Invisible Travelers

Early morning is the best time to see the distant, busy world come awake. Before dawn, with the sun finding them before he finds the world. The criss-crossed ribbons of smoke five miles above are turned to neon ice from behind while we drink our coffee, sit on the step and smoke, looking to the east.

Dozens of contrails already streak the sky, turning reddish and pink and changing shades of pastel fire.

In one of the busiest flyways anywhere, all the overcrowded metal tubes leaving Newark, Philadelphia, La Guardia, Kennedy, Boston for Tokyo, San Francisco, Seattle, Beijing and LA. pass silently overhead.

But sometimes sleep won't come, and I also sit on that step in the quiet hours. The day's high travelers are still somewhere else, and the sky is serene.

The crescent moon is already nearly set, the Seven Sisters of the Pleiades wink in their cold, virginal nunnery, wanting to pull a cloak around themselves for warmth. Orion is in its winter place, militant, telling me the cold months are coming soon,

But sometimes, two or three hours past midnight, when the trucks on the distant interstate are quiet, the hum and puzzle of restless humanity staggers into fitful, resentful sleep, I can just make out, faintly, tweets and calls, carried on the cold air from hundreds, or maybe a couple of thousand feet overhead.

Some nights there are none, but some nights there is a steady feeling of a dark river moving above, and, sometimes, the noise is clear enough to tell who's up there.

Last night, it was a flight of Canada Geese ploughing the air to the south, to winter feeding ponds in Louisiana, in the rich mangrove swamps of Florida, the Sea Islands of coastal Georgia.

I don't know all the calls, and at night there aren't a lot of them. It's a serious business, after all. Nothing to sing about, flying on through the night, thousands of miles.

Just some calling and response. Just enough to make sure that the flock is nearby, and safe, that you're safe, headed in the right direction. Do nothing more to let a lone human--sitting in the dark far below, looking through laboring wings and bodies of invisible travelers at the stars–know that thousands are passing.

But I imagine buntings and Baltimore orioles, scores of streaky brown song sparrows, and dozens of jewel-toned warblers--
Northern parulas, black-throated greens, magnolias, and all the rest.

I've learned that songbirds migrate at night, in great rivers, But they do not sing. Not then. Singing comes later.

But for now, they're leaving us, heading to warmer waters, plentiful food, easier living. Rest.

Singing is better on a branch in the warm sun of the tropics, sipping the sweet juices of some overripe mango, or tasting the white meat of a succulent nut, feeling the thrill of life, the search for a mate, the joy that bubbles up unbidden when wheeling above a sun-splashed sparkle of blue and green.

I can sense them flowing past, tonight, and it saddens me. There aren't as many as there were a few short weeks ago. Winter will be here soon, and there's no changing that. But they'll be back in the spring, full of tales of adventures, Their song will be of the great wheel of life, of the turning of the seasons, of renewal that comes after a testing.

I hope it's not too long. I will be waiting.

Alley Time

I walked the dog at dusk down the alley behind our house last night. It was just after the sun had slid behind the mountain and the light shifted to that peculiar deep shade where daytime things start fading into the shadows.

The growing gloom entices the frightened from their burrows, and we hear the quick shuffling of the leaves as a critter darts, stops, listens, darts, stops, eats, listens for sudden death. The dog hears other things I cannot, and strains against the leash, blood rushing to her ears, hunter's heart quickening. If I let her loose, she would visit swift destruction on anything too slow to escape. It is her nature.

I sympathize, but keep her tethered, sympathizing with those potential victims more.

The wide, quiet back yards exude an air of solidity and age, guarded by huge oaks and elms and Copper Beech and towering, dour Hemlocks. They show a different face than the fronts do. Back here, there is less grooming, less concern with status and social norms. Here, tools are left leaning against sheds to rust by older residents no longer able to care. Here, the grass isn't cut quite as often, and Nature has more of a presence.

Old carriage house doors sag against rusting hinges, grass and weeds grow in some yards, and you can read the signs.

There is one place with a brick barbecue pit that is covered by vines and wild bushes, with roots growing through mortar joints weakened by rain and too many winter nights. It has been 40 years since the kids and their cousins and friends grew up there, give or take a decade. The grandkids are already away at college or playing in a rock band, or married and living in Baltimore or California. They don't visit the old people any more.

They did, once. They spent summers there learning about themselves, exploring the same back yard their parent(s) had, basking in the tolerant love of grandparents who learned lessons the hard way. But the visits gradually slowed until they stopped altogether, and the laughter of children stopped.

The grandparents have grown old, and maybe one has died, but the vines and wild overgrowth says they no longer believe in parties in the yard in the summer night, when children's excited cries bounced off neighbors' houses from a game of hide-and-seek in a pretend jungle full of scary possibilities.

The adults in that remembered, lost time sat in a circle of chairs with drinks in their hands, talking about football and schools and trips and heartbreaks and that cousin or sister everyone thinks is crazy. Those nights when a picnic table was loaded with food everyone has brought, flickering torches made shadows dance on the canopy of leaves overhead, on the lilac bush by the corner of the house. The scene could have been from an ancient campfire on the Mongolian plain, or in the forests of Europe 10,000 years ago, and only the clothes would be different.

The smoke from the bricked fire, the smell of roasting steaks and hotdogs and hamburgers and sweetcorn kept some bugs away and drew others to the feast, and made the children hungry enough to come in from the game, complaining about someone who cheated, and scratching at mosquito bites.

I stopped last night by the ruins, felt the passage of time, and savored the way life's sweetest times are so fleeting, and all the sweeter for that, in that relentless, broad, slow flow of the river of the present into the future.

The dog wants to follow a scent into the underbrush, but I tug on the leash and she gives up and trots down the alley ahead, head down, looking for something to chase. It is her nature.

A Prickle of Hedgehogs

What a prickle of hedgehogs we are,

Ultimately alone, denying the brutal reality of that,

Compulsively looking for love,

For warmth and deep tenderness,

For a touch that says "Come to me. I see you as you are."

For a look that says

"Let's mix it up but good, buster!

Let's leave the sheets damp, the room smoldering and the neighbors jealous."

All the while bristly with defenses: automatic, deadly.

When we are close enough, and when the sheets have dried;

When we're drinking coffee and cursing traffic jams;

When silences grow; when unknowns press against the window,

There come under the door the sounds of small clawed feet,

Snuffling old things, blind and dangerous things.

Things we'd rather keep hidden.

From ourselves.

From each other.

What a prickle of hedgehogs we are,

Driven together, driven apart, dancing on the points

And finding a way.

Sanctuary

The poet Rumi advises us to find a place
high in a nearby tree to hide our spirit.
It is so easily bruised and, when it is hurt,
we cannot hear what it has to say.
I read this and had a question--
why did I wait so long to do the work?

I didn't know how to protect my spirit yet,
to shelter it in that old Hemlock tree there,
massive, dark, unmoving, quiet,
and happy to give my spirit sanctuary,
as though it grew all those years for
no other purpose but this.

Expensive Mistakes

An old printer has sat in the dark

In my oldest's neglected closet

For seven years,

Broken

Barely usable for a year

Before it was replaced.

$400 was the cost. I remember things like that,

Which tells you something...

Mainly that my parents survived

The Great Depression and WWII,

And it was "waste not, want not,"

Every damned day.

If I were to throw that printer out,

It would mean admitting that I spent

Unwisely.

I can hear the disapproval even now.

Expensive mistakes have taught even me, finally.

A printer isn't the worst of it, as much as

Falling hard for the wrong person,

(And who hasn't done that?);

Or falling for the right person at the wrong time,

Or failing to see moments of joy inside pain;

Or not learning that true courage means acting despite great fear.

Or living too much on the surface of things;

And choosing blindness to the gift that is each day;

Or letting life make me ever smaller inside,

Instead of choosing the wisdom of wide arms,

Embracing the passing parade while it lasts.

The printer in the closet needs to go,

Because even expensive mistakes

Must be forgiven.

In The Beginning

You won't live remembering starvation and

Fear of the End. Of. Everything.

You won't know how blood spread across the world

From the swords of tyrants,

Twice, and spawned the thought that maybe

Too many of us just didn't want to live any more;

I fear you may remember other things.

But you won't remember when the world

Stared for decades at the glowing nuclear mouth of Hell

Transfixed. Seduced. Blinded.

But not humbled, even after all that.

But hoping. We know it's a feeble lie.

You won't know that for a while.

You shouldn't know the unending cruelty

Of one to one, many to many, none to one.

That last when a shell of a human is

 forsaken, and utterly alone.

But you will. Humans haven't changed.

Not yet. Not yet.

Not yet, by God.

But you will know other things that I will never see.

Blood-red morning skies filled with smoke

Blown in from endless fires to the west;

Diving tours to the old Key West Shoals,

floating shallowly above old Hemingway's flooded house;

safari tours to deepest, darkest Virginia;

you may stay in a beach house at the edge of

the cliffs of the Blue Ridge Mountains shore;

Ride over the dunes of the Great Nebraska Desert.

Your newness makes me realize

that the smells and sounds of a spring

in the Alleghenies may be passing

At least for now. I want to stop the clock

For you, before you know.

To preserve some tiny spark of this

Divine innocence, this spark of the Divine.

And squeeze it into you, down to your core

So you can carry it with you always.

Until you find it and set it free again,

Always new.

Just like you.

Thunder Comes

One day you're thinking about ordinary things,
Groceries, taxes, walking the dog, the upcoming weekend,
Problems a friend is having, plans to celebrate a graduation,
Finances, cleaning out the garage,
And all the plans... places to finally see, things we put off
Until the kids were launched, safe.
Then we hear thunder over the horizon,
Like the pounding of many hooves,
And the sky darkens, the air grows cold,
the sun loses all warmth.
The pounding, the thunder, the messengers' announcement
Comes up through your feet, sinks into your bones,
and you know what it is.
Fear grips your heart, you clutch each other in silent recognition.
Again. Again. Not again, dear God. Not again.
Plans change with one phone call,
Plans are such feeble things, rattled so easily
By the sound of thunder,
Thudding hooves coming this way. There is no escape.
Let me hold you tight, whisper in your ear the words I dreaded
I'd say again: "I've got you. I'm here. We have to saddle up again. The hurricane will be upon us soon.
There isn't much time."

Hunger

How cruel these nights, his belly knows,

Through rocky valleys filled with snows;

His watchful eyes like shards of ice,

The lonely hunter's hunger grows.

On solitary trails of white,

In empty days and bleakest night,

Ten million nights have come to this,

Death strikes true, or life takes flight.

A feathered hunter watches near

Taunts "Who is that who founders here?

"Who is it damned to roam the rocks,

"While I soar free and without fear?

Red in tooth, sharp in claw,

Ruthless Nature tests us all.

Eat or die, win or lose,

Five billion years, that's been the law.

Yet we believe, against mere fact,

Our charms will make the fates retract

What may just be our final act.

What may just be our final act.

Hope

Sometimes there's nothing to go on but hope.

No proof, no guarantees. No winning lottery ticket. No rescue in the nick of time. No heroes to fix everything in a perfect 42-minute format, just after the last commercial.

Just hope. Just the kind of desperate courage that comes from nothing left to lose. Like me and Bobby McGee.

Maybe it's the days in late winter when it begins to feel like nothing is going to thaw. Something quickens despite all the evidence, Despite all the weight of cold experience. Something feels the long rhythms, Something stirs in the depths of cold nights. Something that has been asleep, but shivers awake, when the moment is right.

Hope.

That's all there is. That's all there's ever been. Foolish, delusional, ridiculous, irrational hope. Something no one can steal. When everything else is stripped away, when everything is gone, and you don't even have a psychic quarter left to make a phone call (and there aren't even any pay phones left, anyway.)

But there's something.... something down there.

Do you feel it, too?

Maybe. Just maybe.

http://youtu.be/ZK4LjURtaDw

We've Done What Was Asked

Jib sweeps the horizon, wake's a long bubbling flow,
Storms uncounted I've weathered, bleak terrors I've known.
My passage, I see, leaves no trace at all.
What good is't to linger, then the words: "Let it go."

The ship sluices onward, destination unknown,
Taut cables weave 'round me, they sing, snap and moan,
Mast bends, prow plunges, new gusts arrive,
The water's hiss climbs, the sea knows her own.

Through the darkness she takes me, my eyes crusted blind,
Brine's coated me, it seems, for three times out of mind.
I pray for the sight of rare stars thru mist,
And dream fitfully of old friends left behind.

Each dawn brings the thought, despite what is past,
We'll find calm water and fair shore at long last.
Still, my body is one with the ship 'neath my hand,
Both battered and worn, we've done what was asked.

Yes

Yes to the unknown, the tears, the sweat.
Yes to the 'morrow-rise and sunset.
Yes to the voices, young and strong,
Yes to the children learning right from wrong.

Yes to the starlight, high and cold,
Yes to the mists, and the mysteries they hold.
Yes to the hard road, traveled alone,
Yes to the love that heals to the bone.

Yes to the losses that each must bear,
Yes to the life sources, sea and air,
Yes to the pains that teach us strength,
Yes to the spirit that wins at length

Yes to the people, yes to strong backs,
Yes to their yokes and labor and acts.
Yes to the toilers, loafers and apes,
Yes to the tillers of history's landscapes.

Yes to the dawn, arms spread wide,
Yes to the rains and winds and tide,
Yes to the future, right or wrong,
Yes to the others, who rise in song.

Inspired by Carl Sandburg's "Chicago Poems"

The Gods Must Change

"One day things will change."

"One day *men* will change."

"But first, Alexander, the gods much change."

DANCER

Grace is a Verb

Numinous Beauty,

Lithe embodiment of Grace.

Stay with me a while.

DANCER

Woman

Rooted in the Earth,

Yearning for Heaven's blessing

Strength. Desire. Woman.

Dancer

Sacrifice

Helpless, wings frozen,

Purity speared by sin

Gift I cannot hold

Ride the Cresting Salt

Ride we the curled, cresting salt;

Cling to a horse of foam;

Drift we through warm waters

Rotten with flowers,

Float we, on a phantom, on

Hope

On Grace.

Wonder

Under the endless heavens,

We, made of those very stars,

Breathe wonder and awe.

Dance the Dawn

Awake ye fertile spirit: Rise!

Dance us into dawn, Spark fire with your thighs.

Conjure the face of the sleeping sun,

Dance away Darkness; Banish her lies.

The Hanging Road

The rider and horse moved onto the narrow path into the wilderness, to Cloud Peak,

In the mountains of the Big Horn sheep, to where the Old Ones hold council.

Her hooves were sure--More sure than his heart. This
She sensed, so the big brown mare gave him loan of hers.

Her breath blew in gusts as the path steepened and the air thinned.
The shadows of the pines grew darker, the air chilled.

The day sank into the west behind the peaks, hour on hour, step by step,

Into the camp of tomorrows, into the undiscovered country.
Up through tendrils of mist that writhed around the trees as though alive.

The spirits of the ancestors hovered at the edge of sight and climbed with them,
The mare seemed to see them, at times. She nickered, and tossed her head.

The rider knew she saw what he could not, so he called out as though to friends.

"Tisane né next ohtse? Tisane n´tao;séxhétséohtse?"
"Where have you come from?" the rider called out in the old tongue.
"Where are you going?"

The only answer was a whisper and a disturbance in the mist,
A rushing of invisible things upward toward the peaks.

The word had been passed, as things are in the spirit world.
The rider was moving up and into the past,

And the trees, the tall trees, seemed wreathed in phantoms,
As though time travelers growing up from the millennial ooze.

In those times, counted in the many hundreds of centuries.
To when the People first stood here, and up there, upon the sacred mountain,

Made sacred because of the soul-work of climbing into the clouds,

Sacred because small men yearned to rise above the world below,
To stand under the Hanging Road with all pride left along the way,

To learn if the owls carried messages from the Camp of the Dead.
The rhythmic metallic thump of shod hooves on granite and dirt

Was now echoing, very faintly, with the distant sound of drums.

Soft at first, the drumming grew in time and harmony,

And the rider heard the singing, the ancient, lilting songs of the Old Ones

Rising and falling in penetrating tenor tones, but always in time
With the steady sounds of the hooves on rock, and of the drums.

He inhaled the drumming, let the singing weave itself into his chest,
Feeling them pull on deep parts of himself, speak peace to his wounded heart.

Through half-closed eyes shadowy forms walked in and among the
Lodgepole pines that crowded the path. They were in their

Summer loincloths and low moccasins, and the drumming
Seemed to both come from them and yet also from the very air.

The mists swirled, formed into the shapes of warriors
And dissolved, the air pulsing to the singing, to the rhythms of the drums.

A figure with jet-black hair long down its back, separated from the others and came close.
A scabbard of intricate bead work crossed the chest, a buffalo skull on its head.

They locked eyes and he saw that the other's were empty sockets, black
As the night sky, and as he looked they filled with stars.

The stars of the Hanging Road, this messenger's eyes,
Two black portals that grew and merged with the vastness above.

The singing and the chanting swelled.
He let his body roll with the rhythm of

The drums and voices, and with the undulation of the horse's back under him.
They escaped the tree line into a meadow broad and dark, shining

Under the whirling cold light of a billion-billion stars,
Stretching away in all directions, the infinity of heaven displayed

In all its awful and humbling glory. The night was absolutely
Clear and pure, clean and still, the isolation absolute, yet
He entered into the solitude and felt his soul soaring up,

Freed at last from earthly things, flying up into the infinite
Oneness below and around, under the Hanging Road.

The mare stopped on her own, perhaps feeling the faintest
Lightening of her burden, knowing she had come to the end.

The drums stopped and the absolute silence calmed her,
She sniffed the air, her ears twitched and she bent to eat.

A messenger streaked across the face of the Deep, rejoicing.
A lost soul had been on a long journey, but was finally home.

The Future is Pregnant

With me.

With you.

She's holding her belly,

Aching,

Hoping we

Change the world,

When we become fully ourselves.

Celebrate the Temporary

Stories of loss, regrets, anger and pain,

Humanity sloshing through gray days, numb to what might be,

Stuck in what was. Second thoughts always.

Years.

Disappointments. Loneliness.

Dreams gone first sour, then withering.

But then hope reappears,

Wiser, cautious, tentative,

But hope nonetheless.

The past lingers like the smell of a dead mouse in the walls,

Gradually fading, but sickening. Hidden, but everywhere.

But hope says…maybe….

Maybe it can end. Hope says open the windows.

Open the windows and doors,

Feel the sun on your face,

Embrace the pain and fear,

Hold it close and forgive all your mistakes.

Forgive all. That is your only escape.

Winter is but a season

All things change.

Even this.

Everything is temporary.

Effort and Simplicity

"The only things that matter in this life are effort and simplicity," the monk told me. We sat a short distance apart on an ancient wall made of massive, moss-covered hand-shaped block of stone as big as coffee tables.

At least, I seemed to be me.

I was different. Completely different, but still me. My soul was the same. Dreams are like that, dreams from another lifetime, particularly. Strange but normal, too. I didn't seem to care.

I gladly sank into the world of long ago.

I was eating the only meal I'd had that day. There was a deep pool of clear water beside the wall. I could see to the bottom, where, a foot or two under the still surface, two hand tools someone had lost, or discarded lay. I reached down with water up to my shoulder and retrieved one and set it dripping on the flat top of the wall. It seemed important to pull it out and let it dry. Someone might need it. That's when he came to sit beside me.

I was exhausted, but exhilarated. Whatever rice and sauce I was eating was hot and good. I shoveled it into my mouth with my fingers.

The day had begun far away, hours earlier. I had been in a race of a sort, with what seemed like hundreds certainly many dozens of people. That part seemed kind of changeable. Some looked like Westerners, but most were from all over the world, of all colors and sizes and ages. Women and children, too. Old men and women shuffling with staffs. There was a feeling in my chest of joy of the running through jungle, up and down ravines through heavy brush, across bare rock headlands and hillsides, then plunging back into the heavy jungle again. I looked down once and realized with a shock that I was a woman, with the diagonal strap of a backpack running between my bare breasts. That was a surprise, but again, it didn't seem to matter in the heat of the jungle, and the animal thrill of running. Others were more or less clothed, but no one seemed to notice. I realized this was a different me, in a time long since passed. Some door in my head, some deep-down locked portal had fallen open, and I had fallen in.

My fellow-racers and I existed only in the moment and for the thrill of the run.

My heart nearly burst with joy, and I quickened my pace.

Everything was lush and vibrant around me. I felt more alive than ever before; every cell in my body tingled with an almost divine energy. The race had begun in the crowds of an old city in India, somewhere in a region I knew as Gujarat. If it doesn't exist in modern times, it did a thousand years ago in the southwest part of the subcontinent. I just knew that somehow.

We left the city in a large group, everyone focused on finishing the race. Soon, we were into the woods, the deep jungle, and the crowd of runners thinned out as some moved ahead and some settled into a slower pace.

The sun was hot in the open, but mostly I ran lightly through tall shade, feeling strength coursing through my body. Barefoot, thick leaves protected my feet as I ran under massive trees, through the understory of thick vines and bushes, often with the path nearly disappearing. Other runners were all around me at times, but I usually could see at least one or two. We waded streams and ran under waterfalls, and the calls of monkeys and raucous, colorful birds cheered us on. I passed old people who shuffled along, waving cheerfully to me as I passed. One such was an elderly woman in her peasant sari, wide hips rolling underneath, a cane steadying her progress. "Ayii, daughter! You are swift on this day! Run! Run faster!"

And so I did.

It went on like this all day. We never stopped for rest or food. But by early evening, the pace slowed, and we clustered at the bottom of a slope covered in deep leaves, with a cable running down it at waist height, like a tram line, or, as it turned out, the handrail of an escalator. It was moving up, as was the whole leaf-covered slope.

We stepped in small groups on the magical moving tramway, held the cable and glided up, glad finally to be able to rest. At first, I still tried to run, but a man behind me chuckled and said: "don't run now, daughter. Let it take you."

At the top was a wide plateau that disappeared into the distance in all directions. It had stone walls and paths, stone buildings covered in moss and vines with tile roofs. Everything had a feeling of immense antiquity.

Under a gigantic forest canopy all was cool and quiet and serene. People moved at a walk now, talking. We headed to a building where we would get food. On the way I passed a towering statue of the Buddha, seated in the lotus position on a platform as big as a modern city block. It must have been eight stories high, seemingly carved from one piece of stone. I experienced a moment of an intense

spiritual feeling. The entire scene turned white for a few seconds and I felt peace spread inside that I've never felt before. It passed after a moment, and I leaned over and pressed my forehead against the statue's base. It felt alive, but moving at a pace of geologic time far beyond my comprehension.

I followed others into a low building, got my bowl of food and went back outside. I was in a state of wonder at all that was around me, found my way to a place on that stone wall away from the others, and sat down.

As I was eating, the monk joined me. I did not hear him. He wore a long, dark simple grey robe with no adornment. He seemed more Japanese than Indian, both in appearance and garb. He carried a folded paper fan in his left hand. His skin was light brown and his hair, cut not overly short, was black, as were his eyes. He carried himself with reserve and dignity. When he sat, he became utterly still, so much so that things around him seemed to slow, too, even the air. He was out of place, but still not alien.

He sat for a moment, watching, impassive, as I picked the tool from the water and laid it beside me on the flat stones. It was a two-bladed hand tool for digging, one side a sharp pick, the other flat-bladed like an adze. I watched the water dripping from the tool on the broad stone of the wall, made of blocks that were three feet on a side, and ate without thinking. I felt his presence, but did not look at him.

When he spoke, his voice was quiet, but strong. He had watched me for a while, and gazed at the dripping tool beside me, then said "The only things that matter now are effort and simplicity. This you now know." And then he was gone.

And So It Begins Again

And so it begins, again,

that urge to shrink from

the cool touch of machines;

the hushed offices,

the looks of concern,

the competent compassion.

Maddening, imprecise precision--

"the blood test found something, we

need to do more tests.....

something's there

on her scans..."

a blurry, thicker patch there,

spots on bone, lung, breast, too.

Interesting words,

"a few places lit up,"

that shouldn't have,

like flying at night over

isolated ranches

in Wyoming, aglow

in the darkness below

with a deceptive warmth.

The needles

and knives,

the gowns,

sensors, drips, monitors,

paper and plastic--

the whole enveloping system,

circling, probing, injecting,

sampling, testing, tasting

a body for disease

like a benevolent, curious,

implacable octopus,

Sorting unknowns from the known,

translating the chemistry

of death and life

into columns of numbers,

leaving it to others to

understand, to face

the ugly chasm between,

where we wait,

naked and afraid, to

learn how it will be to

live. Or not.

And so it begins.

Ordinary Days

She had wanted to
sell the house.
She thought
he'd go first
leaving her alone.
Everything happens
on an ordinary day.
A plane full of
families falls out of
a clear blue sky.
A young mother dies on
a country road after dropping her
daughter at school.
A diagnosis changes everything,
dropping without warning,
from a clear December sky.
He wakes before dawn,
listens to her breathing,
The sky's still dark.
All the years of
ordinary days have come
to this.
What will it be like,
he wonders, to
walk through these rooms
when her voice is silent?

Lazarus, After

Lazarus never smiled

after he rose from the dead.

For 30 years, until he died again,

he was haunted by the

unredeemed souls he saw

in the four days he

journeyed in the afterlife.

Laughter died stillborn in his chest.

That was what he told neighbors—

when he talked about it.

But, it was hard to speak, and

had been since that day.

His throat was always dusty

and his tongue thick.

He was locally famous, though,

and had to play the part

the disciples designed for him.

"Come, Lazarus, tell the people

what happened to you!"

Peter would say.

John would just shake his head

and turn away in pity as

Lazarus forced words

of testimony past

the dust of the tomb

in his throat.

After all, the redeemer of

the world had made him

the only other man,

beside himself, to come back

through the veil. That

came with certain obligations,

they reminded him.

Nothing's as convincing as an eyewitness.

He was always bone cold, though,

and sat in the sun for hours.

He bruised easily, and cuts wouldn't heal

And there were the

aches and pains

from lying on a stone

slab, slowly decaying, for

four days. The crucifixion

came too soon, and

these complaints never

could be addressed.

30 years he lived

before dying again.

Dreading the meeting of those

souls again, explaining

he couldn't help. That the

one who could had

gone on ahead to the

big time, leaving poor

Lazarus behind to play a part

and to sit in the sun.

He forgave that, though.

A miracle is a miracle.

What else could he do?

He only wished his friend had

left behind a few more instructions

for what he was to do after.

Epiphany

I knew a guy,
Cancer survivor,
but worn down by it
to the lacy bone.
Thin, with a dry look.

Still, a light shone through
his parchment skin
like a flame through
a mica shade,
some kind of
organic fire.

The brush with death
left a calling card.
"I'll be back" it said.
"You won't know when."
He knew what
it meant to nearly end.

But there was this
glow, as though
he had a mandate to
slap the shit
out of whatever

was left of his life.
As serious as
a heart attack,
he was—
Afraid of
being forgotten,
Of not being *worth*
remembering—
but determined.

It doesn't have to be cancer.
Could be a stroke,
the kind of thing,
you try to explain,
but which civilians
can't understand:
"I could hear the whine of the bullet,
the ugly sound of
something ruthless
hunting, meaning to kill."

You only know this
if you've heard the whine.
But it misses, now and then.
You realize
you've got bonus time,
but fear being forgotten;
you've wasted so much time....

It now seems important

to slap the shit

out of untruths.

Make some noise.

Burn some rubber.

Find something beautiful.

Make someone cry,

Make someone happy.

Be honest.

Be true.

Repent wasting

each second.

You know not the hour or the day.

It's an epiphany, of sorts,

hearing death whiz by.

It lights a manic fire.

But you live sweeter,

cleaner,

bathed

in that holy light.

Mileposts

There is no knowledge without sacrifice

In order to gain anything, you must first lose everything.

Before I can hope for solutions,

I must first identify the problems.

As an ancient voice cried out

in another time of great upheaval,

much like our own:

> "The oceans have dried up
>
> The mountains crumble
>
> The pole star is shaken
>
> The gods perish.
>
> I am a frog in a dry well. "

There are no solutions

The problems remain.

I pay attention to this.

Endings

It's easy to see the beginnings of things,
not so easy to see the endings.
With eyes like cameras,
the silent guide
can tell you things
you will not believe.
We look at each other and,
confused by guilt and grief, cannot see.
The explicable has ended...
inexplicable things
lick our cheeks in the dark.

These moments
come as from a glimpse
in an old news clip,
some moment of
grace past that is no more,
is swept away and lost.
We lived through the crumbling
of the walls, so sudden
we almost miss it;
that brief, shining moment forgot,
and mere anarchy
and wanton destruction
is loosed upon the world.

An age is ending.
The center has not held.

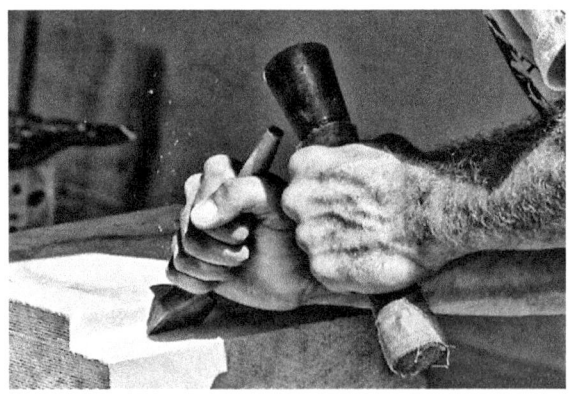

www.ingramcontent.com/pod-product-compliance
Lightning Source LLC
LaVergne TN
LVHW011725060526
838200LV00051B/3025